CW00495700

SOME OF THESE STORIES ARE TRUE

SOME OF THESE STORIES ARE TRUE

Maurice Devitt

Doire Press

First published in 2023

Doire Press
Aille, Inverin
Co. Galway
www.doirepress.com

Layout: Lisa Frank
Cover design: Tríona Walsh
Cover art: Eugenio Mazzone @ unsplash.com
Author photo: Teresa Elford

Printed by Clódóirí CL
Casla, Co. na Gaillimhe

ISBN 978-1-907682-96-4

We gratefully acknowledge the support and assistance of The Arts Council / An Chomhairle Ealaíon.

CONTENTS

for Teresa

Still Dreaming of Livorno

When I was seven I acquired my first chicken,
a Black Italian Leghorn, stolen under cover of darkness
from the coop at the end of a neighbour's garden
and secreted in a wicker basket under the bed.
As I slipped its first egg into the fridge, I remarked
to my mother how I had been woken by a noisy skiffle
from the hen-house next door, followed by the plaintive cry
of a fox, taking care to quickly dismiss an errant feather
from my school jumper. Some days later, when I felt the coast
was clear, I decided to introduce the chicken to my family,
explaining how I had found her wandering in the woods
behind the house and how she had followed me home.
She settled in quickly, sitting beside me on the couch
while I watched cartoons and Aardman re-runs,
scratching industriously around the schoolyard,
even nestling on a windowsill, listening intently,
as the teacher discussed questions of causality,
origin and sequence. And every day a single white egg
until, three weeks in, I found her watching an episode
of *Countryfile* on the pros and cons of battery farming
and her rhythm stumbled. Her eyes grew cold, she skipped
her daily dust-bath and passed the time staring at the sky.
One morning I woke to find her bed empty,
save for one last egg, a sad face etched on the shell.

May 29, 1968

Early evening: after swimming hour at Marian Baths —
Aer Lingus staff and families — I'm perched
in the passenger seat of our blue Volkswagen Beetle,
wet togs and towel tucked like a Swiss roll under my arm,
taste buds primed by the lick of hot vinegar emanating
from the fat paper bag at my feet. We chase the leaking
evening light northwards across the river, sewing-machine
engine straining up Washerwoman's. Into the driveway,
door bursts open and I'm gone, hopping from foot to foot
on the step, eager to claim my position, cross-legged
on the lino, picking at lukewarm chips from a striped blue
and white plate. Couch and chairs filling around me,
I see nothing but a Beatled sprite ghosting across the screen,
his goal an image that still makes me cry.

The Wages of Fear

For years you worked in the shadow
of a man who knew your honesty
was a weakness, who would fleer
at your words, turn certainty
into doubt and scar every weekend
with a cast-off quip,
as he passed laughing through the office
on a Friday evening.

To us a father was all-powerful,
someone to cocoon us on a Sunday night,
read us to sleep, but now I know
how your stomach churned
as a parallel story
played out in your mind.

Salaryman

I might have been fourteen
when I overheard a neighbour
talking to my mother, about how
her husband had been *passed over*
for a job in the bank and him by far
the best candidate. I didn't know
what it really meant, but somehow
I looked at him in a duller light,
this man I was in awe of, partly
because they had all the channels
before us and partly because
he seemed to know the answer
to every question, his didactic commentary
a soundtrack to all our TV viewing.
I began to notice him on later buses
in the morning, his suits less sharp,
his eyes downcast, and then one day
I heard he had retired early.
Walking back from football
in the park, his son explained
that he had left before the company
collapsed and was considering other offers.

Schoolyard Memory

When I refused to share my Latin homework,
you challenged me to a fight
outside the tuckshop, first thing after school.
Having little choice, I accepted,
my strategy hopelessly unclear. You had form,
and news of the mismatch sparked from class to class.

The lane was choked with the cough
of cigarette smoke and the acrid smell of BO
funnelling from the knots of baying boys
heralding my entrance. You strutted around
the makeshift ring, joking and laughing
with your cabal. I was tempted to admit defeat,

but conscious that attack is often
the best form of defence, I walked towards you,
shucking school bag and gaberdine,
baited you with words of bluff bravado,
silencing the crowd and inciting you
to hit me for the first time. I flinched

but didn't react, tried to distract you
with the recitation of random tracts of Latin
unseen, and the declension of obscure French verbs.
You continued your attack, my rubbery mouth
spitting out the syllables of broken words,
until I could take no more, legs buckling under me.

Curled on the ground, I sensed the mood
of the crowd shift to hushed concern,
and unfolding myself like a deckchair into standing,
rushed to concede. *You win*, I mumbled,
sweeping up my school bag and disappearing
into the maw of the crowd, tears starting to fall.

Perhaps chastened by the incipient shock
that rippled through the school, you never asked
for my homework again and, when we left school,
our paths diverged, until today — I saw you in town
stepping out of a brand-new Tesla,
pristine paintwork too tempting to ignore.

Sunday Drive

We were reluctant participants
in that afternoon of separation:
friends swinging on our gate
as they waved us off,
marvellous mysteries that could unfold
on the road and the morning football,
finely balanced at 20-all, now never
to be completed, for when we returned
in the grey sock of evening
family curfews had started to break up
the teams and in the morning,
as we sloped off to school,
our thoughts had already turned
to Heraclitus and how we could never
re-create that moment when posterity
seemed just one jumper's width away.

Black Apples
for Paul Hackett

One day after school we were sitting
on the grass patch at the top of the hill,
watching the *Holy Faith* girls swing by
and filibustering to avoid going home.
You told us a story about black apples —
had read somewhere that after a bite of one
you would never grow old.
There was a tree in Byrne's orchard,
you said, though no one knew which it was.
Set halfway up the road, the house
could be approached from top or bottom,
though we favoured the top — walls lower,
neighbours less athletic and cats more prevalent
than dogs. Suggesting an exploration,
on Saturday night we set off to follow your lead —
squirrelled with difficulty over every wall,
while you sprinted adroitly through the threatening dark,
wiry limbs making light of each new obstacle;
flattened ourselves like starfish every time
a light flicked on, dog barked, or a kitchen door opened.
We channelled Burt Lancaster in *The Swimmer*,
every garden a fresh surprise — slack washing-line,
rusty swing or a rotary mower idling on the upper lawn.
As our eyes lifted above each wall, we locked onto families
circled around the blue screen of the *Late Late Show*,
alert for houselights suddenly turned on or faces
pressed blindly against the glass. You were the only one
who made it into Byrne's, while we were scattered
by a scream into the night, a manically barking dog
and the clatter of bin-lids. We had agreed to meet in the lane
behind your house, four of us waiting nervously
for you to appear. When you did you were breathless,
face scratched, jumper ripped and bounty scarce.
We looked at the apples but none of them were black.

You said you were disturbed before you could find the tree.
Years later, I met you perched at the bar in Tolka House —
you hadn't aged and, I have to say, I was suspicious.

Truth

In my early years,
The Zebra Book of Facts for Boys
was my go-to reference.
Rarely stuck for a capital city, flag,
or element on the Periodic Table,
it was only when, at fourteen,
I brought it as a comfort blanket on my first date,
that I realised its shortcomings:
the conversation flowed
as I sought to impress my consort
with the range of my general knowledge,
but when I left her to her door
and she asked me
if I'd ever kissed a girl before
I didn't know the right answer.

Keeping a Secret

Walking home from school one day
you told me a story,
eyes dark with regret,
as you begged me not to tell.

It hovered for years
at the forefront of my mind,
even pushing itself to the brink
of revelation, when a casual
conversation with friends
appeared to echo your experience.

Though we drifted apart,
I kept my promise.
Now, when I hear from others
what happened to them,
I wonder how you are
and whether I did the right thing.

Antimacassar

I read the word and I'm back there
in the front room, surrounded by cushions
and a powdery silence, flocked walls propped
with display cases of Aynsley and Hummel.
A boy in an adult's world, they have left me
alone in the room, their grown-up lives
orbiting outside. If I hold my breath
I can just about catch short seams
of conversation from the kitchen,
the approaching rattle of delph.
I fear the questions they will ask me,
and how to pitch the answers
to meet their expectations, my shyness
a surprise to be remarked upon later.

Job-Hunting in London
for Catherine

After you've gone a few weeks
and I'm still missing your voice
around the kitchen table,
I imagine you on a red double-decker
between Islington and King's Cross.
Tacking as the bus takes a corner,
you flop sideways
into an empty seat halfway down,
settle your coat
beside you on the banquette
and pull a familiar paperback
from your stuffed cloth bag.
I'd bought it for you just before you left,
knowing you liked the author,
hoping your enthusiasm for the story
would deflect any sense of separation
next time you called.

Parental Guidance

A hot summer's day on the estate, tar-lines
softening in the blistering sun. Constructing
triangles with ice-pop sticks, we meld the corners
with our new liquorice glue, whip them
like frisbees from between our fingers,
watch them ride the warm silent air,
twisting and dipping until they crash and split
like atoms, sticks splayed. I throw one
and it takes off, rising sharply as though from a sling,
stalls like a cough and bounces off
the windscreen of a passing car. Screeching
to a stop, the driver jumps out, engine running.
I am already gone, scooting down the side-passage
of our house. He lopes up the steps, pounds on the door.
No answer at first, just the peripheral view
of a net-curtain settling. My mother opens the door,
her small frame standing tall in the doorway,
face suitably sullen. The man is shouting about what I have done,
while my mother examines the chips in her fingernails.
I appear sheepishly from beneath her housecoat.
He stretches to grab me, she pushes me back,
takes one step forward and explains,
that while she is aware her son is young and reckless,
he doesn't need to feel this anger
to know that he's wrong. Fear will teach him nothing.
The man harrumphs and walks away. I catch
his last regretful glance from the driver's seat,
knowing that this is not over yet.

Victorian Christmas Cake

Every year about this time
I go looking for your recipe,
hand-written and folded
into your *Crosse & Blackwell Cookery Album,*
secreted amongst hundreds of others
of mongrel provenance: clipped
with one continuous motion of a scissors
from a corner of the *Evening Press*;
handouts from a cookery course in Kelly's
with Neven Maguire or torn from the pages
of *Woman's Way* when the dentist's
waiting room was empty.

I've never tried to bake it,
enough for me to unfold the page
and scan, with salty eyes, ingredients
and method, written in your spindly hand —
then you are there, sitting aproned at the kitchen table,
your hair a halo of flour, cup of tea
like a chalice in your hands,
and the smell of mixed peel and whiskey
crowding the room.

Christmas Day
i.m. Michael Kearney 1936-2020

After mass in the Oblates you set your hat for home,
shugging your wren-like frame into your new tweed coat
and scuttling up the Tyrconnell Road,
the walking-stick an essential addition since the fall.
The day is already a tangle of expectation
and, before your lift arrives, you have still to wrap
the Eason's vouchers you bought for your cousins
four weeks ago: the striped paper bag peeping
from the kitchen table, a gentle reminder.
But your days have been busy with dreams of broccoli
and baked ham, the status afforded by a purple paper hat
and the devout silence as your faint, precise voice
reads every cracker joke like a sacred text — fleeting
respite from shadows cast by a coal-effect fire.

The Couch

When it first arrived, the couch was quiet and unobtrusive,
armrests angled perfectly to welcome anyone
passing admiringly through the room, but three weeks in,
it started to assert itself — creeping footprint on the wooden floor,
brush of the velour stubbornly failing to flatten
and, no matter where we placed the lights, we could never
re-create the artful ambience suggested in the shop.

We changed the rug, hoping for an alliance that would settle
the space, but each time we entered, could feel the tension,
as though cross words had just been swallowed
in the nervous silence. We tried cushions of every hue
and texture, only to find them in the morning
strewn randomly around the room, like the aftermath
of a dorm party, invisible guests sleeping it off.

When we painted the walls in a sympathetic tone,
one glimpse sent a ripple of dissatisfaction
through the other rooms, so we simply closed the door.
Now the couch sits squat and menacing in its lair, and we rarely
intrude, unless racing through to pick a piece from the heirloom
tea-set or entertaining unwelcome guests, taking pleasure
in watching them shift uneasily in their seats, before leaving early.

The Dark Art of Plumbing

When he came to fix the boiler, the first thing he asked
was who had installed it, suggesting that not only
would he have to get the boiler working, he would
have to unwind all that had gone before —
loose pipes, Escher-like connections and, worst of all,
a failure to respect the vagaries of water.
He riffed on a theory that getting water
to do your bidding was a rare gift, bestowed
on only the chosen few. Somewhere a radiator gurgled.

The installation had been so long ago
I couldn't remember, so when he was gone
I pulled out the original receipt, most of the ink now lost
to some celestial archive, though I could just about make out
his name scribbled at the bottom of the page.

Summer Pastoral

The weather was so good that I left
a poem unfinished on the desk,
swapped slippers for dancing shoes
and stepped out onto the street.
As I did, every door seemed to open
in sync, disgorging a series
of flawless figures, just about recognisable
as my neighbours, dressed uniformly
in chiffon and silk — greys, blues
and powdery pinks — falling
into geometric formation.

A man passed me a parasol
and I sashayed into the swell,
toes and heels in perfect time
to the lush music that enveloped
the scene, every movement
choreographed to a jaunty rhythm,
smiles appearing on even the cloudiest
faces. When we reached the end of the street
we twirled and bowed in concert,
hats and caps erupting into the sky
as the music crescendoed and started to fade.

Conversation turned to the rumour
that a famous musical director
had bought a house on the road
and we wondered would he really fit in.

The Sisters

After the other guests leave, you are alone
with them, and, in the minutes it takes
for absence to settle, you plump up the cushions
on the settee, stoke the fire — seeking refuge
in the crackle of sparks — and wonder
what direction this might take. Neighbours
and friends for years, there was
that gnawing silence the last time you met,
a silence you just couldn't explain.
Yet, when you invited them around,
they were quick to accept. Now,
turned towards the fire, you sense their eyes
on you — the burr of a cleared throat signalling
a conversation that could go either way.

Autumn

From the car park we take the upper path
above the reservoir, slow our step
until we are shadowing the trees,
shuffle prayerfully along the rising track.

We stop for a moment and listen to the forest
shrug into stillness; the trees circle, whispering
to themselves, tipping over slightly to sense
the rhythm of our breath, as though

it might tell them where we had come from,
why we were there. But we no longer know
the answers to these questions, so say nothing.
A light wind, passing through, coughs

nervously into the silence, prompting
the trees to release a babble of leaves.

Animal Husbandry in Dublin 6

I was a junior counsel at the Beef Tribunal
when I started to dabble, taking a cow
in lieu of cash for my first monthly fee
and, when my senior told me he was moving up
from Ranelagh to Rathgar, I saw my opportunity —
a roomy, red-brick semi on a leafy suburban street,
the perfect environment for a homesick cow.
The garden was small and ornamental, a lawn
the size of a Subbuteo pitch, though,
before I got a chance to simplify the landscaping,
she had already set her eye on the herbaceous
border, the scrumptious shrubs.
Undaunted, I rolled out wall-to-wall grass,
a water-trough in the bottom corner,
walls painted with pastoral scenes
worthy of the French Landscape School,
faux cowbells dangling from the eaves. I think
I was the only cattle farmer on the road, although
I suspect the neighbour four doors down
had started keeping chickens, the rooster
silhouetted on the party wall
against the tempering sun. At first,
I would herd her in the clotted stretch of darkness
just before dawn, switch of hazel in my hand,
nervously clipping my wellingtons.
Later I took to walking her boldly
down the middle of the road, having decided
that hiding in plain sight was a better strategy,
though always careful to hurry her along
if she raised a tail. Initially, the residents objected,
but when I started to provide them with warm, fresh
milk (shop-bought and heated on the stove)
every morning, they were lured into a bucolic dream,
and desisted — her presence on the street less contentious
than the man who parked his branded tradesman's van

on the path outside his house. Now she's getting older,
I notice the laps around the garden have grown slower
and she needs glasses when she watches TV,
but on wet days she still stands trenchantly in the middle
of the green, flank turned towards the driving rain,
her mind filled with guilt for each fresh storm.

Coming Home

One day the key doesn't turn in the lock
and he wonders if he has done something wrong,
if there is something different
about his approach: the way he inserted
the key, the way he turned it
with that customary wiggle, assuming
it would open. He tries again,
confidence draining with each attempt,
and all the little assumptions
built into his process seem shaky.
The nerves in his fingers, so used to success,
now expect failure. Could it be the wrong key?
He pats his pockets — finds nothing
but a comb and a train ticket.
Stands in silence on the doorstep,
as though waiting for someone to open the door.
There should be no one home, yet he listens
for the slightest tremble of sound
and, when he calls to a neighbour to borrow a spare,
a stranger answers — explains
how nobody has lived there for years.

Loitering with Intent

I see him standing in his front garden
pretending to clip his roses,
but know he is waiting to snare me
and I can't turn back now.
He greets me as he settles himself
on the blistered railing, wonders have I heard
the latest about the couple in no. 10,
bemoans the rise in petty crime
since the neighbours' WhatsApp was set up,
then drifts seamlessly into political commentary
and sport. I am watching his lips move
but not listening, I am looking into his eyes,
wondering if his words reflect
what he is thinking or is it that he just wants
to hold on, knowing that when I am gone
the evening light will start to curdle
and he will reluctantly retreat
to a kitchen full of cat food
and a table set for one?

Pearl

Sitting in the small room at the end of the return,
afternoon sloping into silence, I hear
the clip of magpies' heels on the tiles overhead.
My eyes follow the sound, like a scribble on the ceiling,
as they potter in the afternoon heat.
I imagine them tuxedoed, strutting in singles and pairs,
wings folded casually like arms behind their backs —
a welcome respite after a busy day, waking early
to clear moss from the gutters, bickering over food scraps
in the garden — but, all the time, waiting for darkness,
casinos to open, champagne to spill,
jewelled eyes primed for glitter and gold,
beaks sharpened for each opportunity
and, in the morning, a solitary earring on the step.

Détente

When I arrived home, the cat was already packing,
said she had had enough — if not in so many words —
stole a last glance at her coat in the bedroom mirror
and left. Not as much as a purr for a week, though
we noticed on WhatsApp she had been taken in
by a family on the next road, who put up a photo,
thinking that someone might claim her.
We said nothing, although some of the neighbours
drew our attention to the post. *A good likeness alright,*
we acknowledged, *but not our Mitzie*, hoping
that the absence of any desperation on our part
would blow her cover. Then, this morning, the gift
of a squiggling mouse dropped through the cat-flap,
a fitting first foray in what could be a delicate process.

The Landlord

As soon as he's finished painting
the railings, he starts again:
caressing the gloss with a blowtorch,
to see it blister and burst, hot flakes
dropping onto the path outside.
Chisels stubborn maps of colour
until they peel off and he can touch
raw iron, chivvying with a wire brush
to make the metal more receptive.
Only then does he begin to paint —
at least two coats of Hammerite Black.
An old sheet crumpled against the base
of the supporting wall, a cushion
to cradle his knees and a blackened twig
to mix the pot. He is meticulous, using
brushes of various sizes to coax the paint
into reluctant corners, making sure
he doesn't miss a spot. Neighbours
are impressed with his endeavour,
pristine railing surely a reflection
of a palace inside, where tenants wait,
shivering in towels, for the shower to be fixed.

The train driver

who lives next door
has been known to talk in his sleep,
reciting timetables to his wife,
eyes blinking faster
when they enter a tunnel.
He sits up suddenly in bed,
cries out as the wardrobe
hurtles towards him,
his legs straightening
against the footboard as he brakes,
frame sparking and screeching
to a halt, yards from a boy
who used to bully him at school,
scared eyes piercing the night.

Cherry Blossom

For weeks we have waited for the cherry blossom
to bloom, to be surprised again by its predictable beauty.
We mark *hanami* with a glass of champagne in the garden,
as if the year has reached some sort of peak
and will now turn downhill: fallen petals, yesterday's confetti,
plastered to the wet pavement outside.

When it flowers again, we could be one year older,
concertina minds dismissing all that might happen
in-between: early days, waking to the disappointment
of fewer flowers every morning; leaves muscling through
to form a lush sway of green that will carry the summer
and remind us that the joy of life is often to be found
in the comfort of repetition, reassurance of the mundane,
and just the occasional instance of perfection.

Walking

I set off in the confident heat, my destination a secret
even to me. The crossroads at the bottom of the hill
offers three choices: the first looks particularly promising
— straight with a slight incline — although I know
from experience that once out of sight, the path turns
sharply and disappears into itself, a rather frustrating
denouement for the ambitious walker but, on the other hand,
a worthy excuse for a hasty return to the house, on days
when not all my fates are aligned and my *plantar fasciitis*
is acting up; the second is bearded with trees and seems
to funnel into darkness but, after the descent through
the railway tunnel, the road rises briskly, dusts itself off
and opens out into a delta of grassy aspects, each more lush
than the last; the third choice is by far the most enticing,
a set of stout bollards manning a sinuous pathway
that on this frou-frou autumn day seems to be paved
with gold leaf. It leads to what I believe in the distance
is a small wood, abundant with fruit and multifarious fauna.
I have been tempted I must admit, although the Weimaraner
perched on the pillar of the first house is a slight deterrent.
My neighbour went there last week and never returned.
His wife received a letter in his distinctive hand,
reassuring her that he was ok and not to panic.
She has woken in the night to footsteps in the attic
and the front door swinging open,
though she's convinced the events are not connected.

Coffee Morning, Herbert Park

Though it's a cold November day,
the low sun entices them outside
to sit in a scrum around a picnic table,
the lone smoker adrift at the end
of the bench. There is a strict sequence
to their conversation, opening with
an update on their ailments, progressing
to the rugby at the weekend, a roll call
of grandchildren and an update
on former colleagues. As work stories
unfold, the table is divided.
Some, effusive up till then, lapse
into silence, perhaps remembering
what they did, or what was done to them.

The retired magician

sits framed
in the bedroom window,
like a bird in a gilded cage.

Night drops,
a shroud unravelling
to cover the house

and, when the morning sun
unpeels the darkness,

he is gone, a lone dove
perched on the chimneypot.

A Bolt of Happiness

Maybe you thought it would never happen,
maybe you thought you had wished it away.

Then one day when your mind is consumed
by other things — the meeting you are rushing

to, a dress you had seen in Arnotts that was gone
when you went back and the growing list

of people you had promised to call, then promptly
forgot. Stopped at a pedestrian light on Baggot Street,

you are already late and peppering to cross,
when the warm whisper of a breeze circles,

awakens the memory of a boy in a blue denim shirt —
his tousled hair, elegant hands and the day

he first spoke to you that summer — now the air
is still, your mind clear of everything but him.

The Mermaid and the Lighthouse Keeper

Three weeks after the gorse-fire, he notices
fresh growth among the stubble,
fingers of green clawing through the embers
and, when a summer squall whips
like a scarf around the hill, the spines
brighten and the grey ash darkens with rain,
forms runnels down the incline, across
the walking trail, dispersing
into the capillaries of the earth below.
After many years of hiking alone
on the cliff path, he knows that the flowers
will soon appear, flaring yellow
to the fishermen dropping lobsterpots in the bay.
When they are at their brightest,
he will gather enough to make a lavish hand-tie,
wrap them in stalks of lavender
from the kitchen-garden and leave them
on the small outcrop of rock below the station,
beside the metal struts of the old diving-board.
He saw her there, that single time, stretched
on a ledge above the foaming sea,
eyes dazzled by the sweeping beam.

Tricking the Light

He paints in a room at the top of the house
and every morning climbs the arthritic stairs,
one creak at a time,
pauses for a breather on the attic return,
then shuffles up the final few steps.

He ascends in total darkness,
to catch the room off-guard,
eyes taking in the sooty shift
from night to day. Everything
is just as he left it —

the tree he has painted through the window
every day for thirty years, is still there
to reveal the lies in yesterday's work.
He starts the story one more time,
not knowing how it will end.

What Colour are Oranges?

The oranges have waited in the bowl
for almost a week now, a sunny
counterpoint to the dark presence
of the dining-room table. You say
they soften and sweeten before they turn,
and that the ripest fruit is heavy for its size.
I lift one to test its weight, cup my hand
like the dish on a scales, roll the sphere
up my arm, then pop my elbow
to send it arcing back into my hand
(a trick I learnt at school that has gone
criminally unused). I press and circle it
with my palm on the table, like shaping
plasticine, sense the pith pulling from skin,
ligament from bone. I open at the heart
and tear downwards, taking care to undress it
as one seamless garment,
hoping that it's been worth the wait.

The Health Questionnaire

And someday
all the questions I've tended to ignore
will need to be answered,
as my once perfect body
starts to decay, ailment-by-ailment,
and the taut tendrils of my mind
snap, leaving tracts of information —
the much-vaunted fruits
of study and osmosis — stranded
the wrong side of the divide,
and I will no longer know
which to ferry over first,
the fox, the chicken or the bushel of wheat.

The Politics of Waiting

The display at the bus-stop promises five minutes
and I'm buoyed by this speck of certainty
in such a wilful world. Like a television
playing in the background of a busy pub,
I find my eyes magnetically attracted
to the screen, though the mismatch with the timing
on my watch prompts me to question everything
I've ever learnt about the length of a minute
and, while the display may indicate arrival,
the bus turns out to be a *ghost,* slipped momentarily
into the system to boost our hopes
and, just as quickly, *disappeared.* The man
in Central Control decides to further test
our commitment and leave the screen blank,
so I stare at the horizon searching for a blur
that might turn out to be a bus, aware
he is watching, smug in the knowledge
that an unscheduled bus is never late
and each new arrival is a pleasant surprise.

Then

there's the night you are sitting
in the kitchen, house settling
into a timid darkness, and your thoughts turn
to events of the day: the meeting
that didn't go well, the hush in the canteen
when you walked through
and the hours you spent sitting aimlessly
in your office, wondering how things
could have been different
and whether what you said was wrong,
lips repeating with no sound. You reach
for the shutter of sleep, hoping it will scramble
the algorithm for guilt, allow your heart
to open slowly to a torpid morning sun.

In Principle, Peter was Right
after Laurence J. Peter 1919-1990

My boss called me to his office,
that plush, chrome cavern on the ninth,
remarked how my performance had surpassed
all expectation and outlined a position
he would like me to consider. At first, I feigned
disinterest, my gaze apparently distracted
by the precipitous view to the river, but,
not for the first time, the black tongue of ambition
quickly sold me the deal. A corner office on the seventh,
an oak desk the size of a small house, Chesterfield suite
in distressed leather and a green banker's lamp.
I was accompanied by boxes of management books,
bought but never read, and, waiting to crowd the bare walls,
a tower of framed certs, impressive to look at
but not to examine. I called my mother, she called
her friends, and I settled in quickly, my team rapt
and responsive, their lunch breaks spent googling
my career. Deal after deal stacked up, board members
whispered my name, for months I could do no wrong.
Until one day, I'm not sure when, my numbers became
a fraction of themselves, presentations appeared
in invisible ink and every sales pitch
sounded poached and scrambled. I tried harder
and the target moved further away. Friends trawled
my past for torn blankets of comfort, but they covered little
of the gloom. I had grown to believe that failure
was a distant cousin of success, mentioned in passing
at family parties but never seen, yet, when it arrived,
I could hardly tell the difference, and recognition
brought such a glorious release.

Half-Life

When I tried to use my stapler this morning,
I realised it was gummy and the staple box was empty.
So, I bought another pack. Five thousand pieces
it said on the side and, with my eyes unable
to pick out more than twenty without losing focus,
I took their word for it and brought it home.
Only being an occasional stapler myself,
I got to thinking that unless I took drastic action,
these staples would outlive me, presenting
the additional problem of including them
in my will, a task that was not as easy
as it seemed. Would I leave them as a pack
to a younger person, only coming into
staple-using years or would I divide them up
into smaller boxes, to be taken as mementoes,
both of the service and my life? I, of course,
procrastinated and chose to do neither,
pushing them to the back of the drawer,
an unwelcome reminder of my mortality.

There is a story

inside every stone, and so it is for this mossy chock
of granite that has held the gate open for years,
its face a thousand little mirrors. No one knows
how it got there, perhaps kicked up from some
underground disturbance and abandoned
in what was then an open field above the village,
view unobstructed to the sea. In time the house
was built as a bolthole for a gentleman in the city
and someone, frustrated with the wilful swing
of the gate, retrieved the stone from a redundant pile
and nudged it into place against the crunch of gravel,
eyes set to watch everyone who would come and go,
ears growing used to the swelling cacophony
of their brickbat lives, on what was once a quiet street.
But be careful if you wish to discover the hidden tale,
for rashly splitting the stone may lose the thread — it would
be better to wait for a stonemason with the hands of Bernini
to chip away patiently at any needless preamble,
taking time to reveal the story hidden within.

It Might be Over

This morning we found
a glass slipper on the step
and, despite me trying
to convince you
that it looked a little tight,
you felt it was a perfect fit
so ever since
I have been watching you
like a hawk, as you hover
in the vicinity of the front door,
though, thankfully, one postman
and two chuggers later,
there is still no sign of a prince.

Neighbourhood Watch

When she woke, he was gone,
scent of him still dawdling
on the stairs, phone
and wedding-ring abandoned
on the console table in the hall.

After three weeks, she packed
his clothes into a suitcase,
left it in the porch.
In the morning it had vanished
except for the shoes he never liked,
perched squarely on the step.

A woman down the road,
dowdy and disinterested
since her last romance,
has been spotted wearing lipstick
to the bin
and the milkman has remarked,
in the form of an open question,
how she's increased her order
from one bottle to two.

Dippy Eggs

I'm looking for a rolling boil,
water lapping the side of the pot.
Time creeps by at first,
then rushes to a moment of decision,
like a golfer putting
in the throes of the yips,
unsure when to release. For everything
there is a perfect point of lift-off.
Missed, and the chance is gone.

Once in
there are four and a half minutes
of waiting, not long enough to do much else,
except ponder
the great philosophical questions
like what came first
or how brown should toast be?
Time that you might think
is lost to the day, but thought
is often its own reward.

Lift out the eggs, settle and sever.
A clean cut around the neck
and the head falls,
yolk a sticky yellow mess,
perfect for dipping.

October Sunday

It's one of those days when you realise
that summer is not coming back,
despite the light bursting confidently
into the bedroom, the deception
of heat behind glass and the glimpse
of a neighbour hurrying coatless
up to church. It's the leaves that give
the game away, and the grass.
You try to convince me it is still growing,
your deft scissors-work a joy to behold.
Only bettered by the pumpkin
waiting on the step,
face you carved a good likeness of me,
eyes casting ruefully into the night.

Degrees of Separation

Today it's your turn to walk
your son to school, stand
on the step in the mizzling dark,
like a paperboy waiting to be paid,
while she prepares his lunch,
straightens the collar on his coat
and issues her final, clipped instructions,
before opening the door and passing him
wordlessly into your world, secure
in the knowledge that she has packed
his favourite sandwiches
and ten minutes talking about the match
will never be enough
to deflect from last night's tears.

An Afternoon in Ruhpolding
for Greg

A trip scrambled together in the dark hours
after the funeral: two months later,
a morning flight to Munich,
train through Traunstein to Bibelöd,
leafy sub-station on the edge of town.
May, and the air is hung with a summer haze,
walkers and shoppers burrowing quietly
about their business, streets and buildings
Truman Show pristine. We drift into a side-room
at Schuhbeck, a coven of seven friends
huddled on bench seats around a wooden table.
First taste of German lager and the conversation
starts; voices, interlaced and animated,
remembering football trips, work, nights out —
familiar stories recited like mantras
of friendship and love, while feelings,
previously unspoken, stutter into being.
Hours pass and the swirling chatter
funnels into a shared silence, arc lights
flickering on the street outside.

World Cup Final 1966, Poulshone Beach
for Terry

We watched on the bulging screen
of a Bush television, set in the corner
of a dark, afternoon living room
that smelled of salad and sea. Our cousins'
clapboard holiday home, marine blue
shutters closed against the sun, we sat
silently on the floor between the legs
of grown-ups who talked as they passed
sandwiches around. At full-time we burst
blinking into the light, to replay the goals
and imitate our heroes. Being slightly older,
my brother had first pick and chose Geoff Hurst,
taking immediate possession of the ball,
while I, a nine-year-old in salt-bleached hair,
who pictured himself as Siggi Held,
reluctantly went in goal and, between shots,
cast a furtive eye on the scorched path
twisting down the hill, hoping to catch
a glimpse of the girl in the blue summer dress.

The Team for Sunday

On Thursday, after training, the team was announced,
pinned anonymously, like a Banksy poster,
to the noticeboard of the local pub. Lost in a thicket
of handbills — winning numbers in last week's draw,
faded league table torn from the pages of the *Evening Press*
two months before, names on the committee
selling tickets for the Christmas dinner dance.
I would zero in from across the room, taking care
not to show too much interest, picking out
tell-tale letters, name-shapes to indicate I was in the team.
Caught in this tangle of apprehension, I offered to go to the bar,
taking a detour past the board. A quiet victory to be named
in the first eleven, and twelve or thirteen would have me
in striking distance. A quick scan, and I slipped out the side-door,
felt the reassuring draft of cold air, dark indifference of the night.

True Romance

Rushing out the door to meet you,
I am already sitting on the bus
when I sense I have forgotten something,
just not sure what. Keys, money, cards,
all present and correct. I kick-start
my memory by silently reciting
the multiplication tables, one to twelve,
mentally slurring the answers
when I'm not sure, but nothing triggers
and, by the time I reach the restaurant,
I've already covered US State Capitals
and half the Periodic Table (a testament
to my mother, her love of *Pointless*).
When I arrive, you are already sitting
at our favourite table — a special night,
months in the planning — your tanned
fingers splayed against the white linen,
and I remember what it is I'm missing.

The Wedding Party
for Jessica & Brian, Mount Juliet, July 16ᵗʰ 2022

You wake early, throw open the curtains to a view
that hasn't changed for years: today you could be
Juliana* and Somerset surveying your demesne.
Mist hangs like a low cloud on the River Nore,
horses are already frisky in their paddocks
and the rolling parkland, lush with oak
and elm, sweeps serenely to the horizon.
Excitement courses through you as you ready
yourselves — Brian, tense and impatient
with cufflinks and buttons, rushes to reveal
his handsome self, while Jessica, a calm and focused
vision in silk, effortlessly unveils her beauty.

Family and friends, giddy for the day,
busy themselves in hotel rooms, or pack
their weekend lives into the boots and backseats
of cars, to drive on ever narrower roads, deeper
and deeper into the Kilkenny heartland —
that mystical labyrinth of hurling, pottery
and glass — until the Mount Juliet estate
opens up to them, offering its splendour and magic.
A lump in the throat as they get closer,
knowing it will be one of the great days.
Honoured to share it, they savour every minute,
as you take your first step towards a flourishing future.

* Mount Juliet was built in 1757 by Somerset Butler, the first
Earl of Carrick, for his wife, Lady Juliana Boyle (aka Juliet)

Breaking the Silence

I hadn't seen her for years so when she sat
in beside me on the morning bus, I wondered
would she recognise me and, if so, how
had she chosen to remember our brief liaison:

flurry of romantic nights in the early weeks,
the concerts that flagged up such extremes
in music taste, or the messy break-up, that,
even now, makes my palms sweat?

I chose to say nothing — headphones on
and eyes staring through a clearing
hurriedly created with a sleeve
on the breathy window. I thought

my assertive indifference was bound
to pre-empt any glimmer of recognition
and, with eyes and ears occupied, I could
easily defend against accusations of being rude.

Still her perfume did evoke certain strains
of historical temptation and it was nice, once again,
to travel the five miles into town, my thigh pressed
to hers. Lost in the hypnotic cocoon of music,

the frayed lyrics and the anthemic beats, I enjoyed
the twenty minutes of her anonymous, dreamlike presence
and, as I excused myself to disembark, she turned
and whispered, *it's funny, I never knew you could sing.*

Puzzle

I was doing a jigsaw of Kinsale Harbour —
rows of candied houses crowding nosily
around the bay — and had just completed
the terrace on Pier Road when you appeared
in the picture, tripping out the door of Actons Hotel
on the arm of a man I didn't know. Cutting through
the freshly laid green, you hesitated at the pier wall,
as though waiting for direction. I had assembled
the edge pieces first, so your options for escape
were limited. Afraid that I might lose you in the labyrinth
of streets behind The Trident, I scrabbled in the box
for the pieces that would lead you on the waterfront
back towards town, having first distracted you
with a jagged island of difficult blue, your eyes
drawn by the first clinking sounds from the marina.
Snapping each piece into place, I managed to stay
one step ahead, while you, like Dorothy in red shoes,
were happy to follow the stepping-stones as they appeared,
wheeling past Dinos, the carpark and onto Pearse Street —
the look on your face when you walked into The Blue Haven,
me sitting in the lounge, jigsaw on the table, one piece missing.

Clearing the House
for Matthew

You open the door,
stop in the hallway to listen,
a fuzzy silence surrounds you.

Pass through the rooms
as though for the first time —
everything looks different
without her:

ornaments, once a concatenation
of trophies from her vibrant life,
cower in their own dust,
nervous lights flicker, uncertain what to do

and family photographs
picked up and studied a hundred times,
are distant and unfamiliar,
reluctant to make eye contact.

You step into the kitchen,
hoping for respite,
to be met
by the tidiness of absence,
all the questions you never asked.

Everyday Dreams
for Gerard

When I arrive
I notice you standing in a corner
of the carpark,
cigarette pinched like a pencil
between your fingertips,
shoe lazily working a pattern
in the still wet gravel.

I hesitate for a minute,
unsure whether you are wrangling
with a seamy problem
from your business day,
or chasing
the chord progression
of a song you've never played.

The Empty House

After you moved to the nursing home
you never saw the house again,
rejecting all offers to drive by or visit.
Afraid, perhaps, that sixty years of joy,
secreted in the chambers of your mind,
would be sundered by an ill-judged return.

The short terrace a beachhead
of developer intent in the hill field,
later swallowed up by the slow creep of housing
down the Tolka Valley. How well you must have
remembered its stout, familiar presence,
the ivy-bearded pebbledash a point of reference

for drivers sweeping up the hill. Starter homes
for newlyweds, families living coincident lives:
children raised, schooled and scattered; parents left
to the shared, yet solitary, role of waiting.
Widowed early, you had long learned to hide
the scars of loneliness and absence,

watching selflessly as we stuttered into our
grown-up world, allowing you to unpack
a new-found freedom like a second life,
until your faltering mobility could no longer be veiled
from a sprightly mind. The idea of a nursing home
snaked its way to the top of a short queue of options

and you resigned yourself to a fresh incarnation.
How seamlessly you slipped into this new role:
confessor and confidante, ground floor room
a busy hub for staff and residents alike,
and you, as you listened and shared advice, were struck
by how often the stories brought you back there.

Unspoken
for Teresa

It must have been long before we met
that you learned the sorcery of silence —
how words only matter when they matter,
and how the breathless scram of conversation
sometimes does little but distract the senses.
I remember one time driving to Connemara,
you said nothing until just outside
Kinnegad — then merely to remind me
how the motorway spurs and not to miss
the turn. I had started the journey
with a skittish collage of jokes
and useless facts, intended to impress
my captive audience, but even these
quickly trailed off into quiescence —
the car a hide from which to stalk
the passing beauty, our breath measured
and perfectly in sync, eyes on fire
and your lips carved into a blissful smile.

ACKNOWLEDGEMENTS

Acknowledgements are due to the editors of the following publications in which versions of some of these poems first appeared: *Abridged, Arc Magazine, Atrium Poetry, Bangor Literary Journal, The Black Nore Review, Boyne Berries, The Cormorant, Dodging the Rain, Drawn to the Light, Dreich, Foxglove Journal, The High Window, HOWL New Irish Writing, Impspired, Ink, Sweat & Tears, The Irish Times, Live Encounters, The Music of What Happens (Purple House), Nine Muses Press, North West Words, Poems & Pictures, Poems for Patience, Poetry Village, Romance Options Anthology* (Dedalus Press), *The Same Page Anthology, Skylight 47, Sky Island Journal, Spilling Cocoa Over Martin Amis, Spillwords*, and to the judges and organisers of the Bangor and Poems for Patience Competitions of which two of the poems were winners.

In the creation of this collection special thanks are due to Amanda Bell, Maeve O'Sullivan and my brother Terry and his 'book club' for their valuable inputs on earlier versions of the manuscript; Brian Kirk and Jean O'Brien; the members of the Hibernian Writers Group, past and present; my brothers and sisters, wider family and friends — too many to mention — who have encouraged me along the way and, of course, Teresa, for her unwavering support and wise counsel.

Finally, thanks to John Walsh and Lisa Frank of Doire Press for their confidence in taking on the collection, and the patient support of Tríona Walsh during the publication process.

ABOUT THE AUTHOR

MAURICE DEVITT, born in Dublin, completed an MA in Poetry Studies at Mater Dei, following a thirty-year career in Insurance and Banking. His debut collection *Growing Up in Colour* was published by Doire Press in 2018. His poems have featured in a significant number of journals, both in Ireland and internationally, and have been nominated for Pushcart, Forward and Best of the Net prizes. He is a past winner of the Trócaire/Poetry Ireland, Poems for Patience and Bangor Poetry Competitions, and has been placed or shortlisted in many others, including The Patrick Kavanagh Award, The Listowel Collection Competition and Cúirt New Writing Award.

Maurice is the chairperson of The Hibernian Writers' Group, and his Pushcart-nominated poem, 'The Lion Tamer Dreams of Office Work', was the title poem of an anthology of the group's work published by Alba Publishing in 2015. He is curator of the Irish Centre for Poetry Studies Facebook page, where he posts featured poems, news and poetry articles on a daily basis.